Diet for Athletes

Lose weight easily

Jacob D. Copeland

Contents

Chapter One

Introduction

What a shambles for the powerful.I became recognized as Jacob D. Copeland from P90X (also known as "P90X Jacob D. Copeland) in 2004, when I was 41 years old.Celebrities and politicians tried P90X and heard my full name many times during the Shoulders and Arms workout, where I appear as a cast member. Tony Horton, the wellness coach behind the program and an old friend of mine, says it several times throughout the activity.People started remembering me all across the world, not just in America. Even in Moscow, Russia, they treated me as if I were their emperor. (I explained that I wasn't Tony Horton, but they seemed unconcerned.) In P90X, I appeared. For them, that was sufficient.)Because I participated in an experimental group for the item and smashed it, the company that made P90X invited me to appear in one of the recordings. P90X really transformed my body, at least in terms of appearance, and I relished the opportunity to show off a six-pack for the first time.However, the narrative does not finish there since... my results were short-lived. I couldn't stand behind it.So far, there have been few people who have tried P90X or another fitness regimen.Can be said in that regard. It's just too difficult, dull, monotonous, or embarrassing; something unexpected often occurs, resulting in a setback.The same can be said about most new diets, gym memberships, and even weight-loss surgery.The weight, like bad habits, returns.We've all seen Oprah Winfrey, Kirstie Alley, and other celebrities yo-yo from obese to not-so-fat and back again despite having access to high-priced fitness trainers and nutritionists. It's embarrassing, but it highlights a shameful fact about the great majority of these diet and exercise plans: Most people see improvements at first as their bodies adapt to a favorable intervention, but they eventually drift back to where they started, dubious, perplexed, and disillusioned.In my case, I regained all of my pre-P9oX weight, lost muscle, and saw a rapid decline in overall wellness and fitness.I tried to recover with additional P90X 90-day cycles and, surprise, started a web-based fitness program.Even though the pendulum swung back to unremarkability each time, workout support gathering remained on pace.From P90X Joe to Average Joe, I went through a transformation.My regrettable peculiarities and advanced age were not just catching up with me. They had a good lead. The wheels finally came off in 2012, when I was 49 years old.In a yoga class full of athletic females, including my lovely date for the day, whom I thought may be a guardian if she stopped calling me and everyone else "darling," I was maintaining my ground. (That irritated me, but I have a different point of view...)The world started to spin before my eyes like a film in fast speed as I completed the final sit-up and symbolized a few separate phrases, serenades, or heavy breathing.What the f-ck was going on, I had no clue. I couldn't remember which direction I was dealing with at the time. The chamber was almost as hot as a sauna, yet I became chilly and nauseated almost immediately.Only one item was checked out—kneel down before I fall over.I'd also had four pieces of Kentucky Fried Chicken before to class and had no desire to see it again. No, God no. This isn't the time.I closed my eyes in an attempt to halt the twisting, but it didn't work right away. In my head, the movie continued to play like a nightmare.I simply sat there, perspiring profusely and looking as white as a ghost, trying to get through it.I was a catastrophe zone by the time I was able to withstand escalating with the help of my pals. I moved and looked like a frail senior citizen on the verge of passing away.It was humiliating, unpleasant, and frightening to say the least.The yoga instructor wondered aloud whether she needed to call for assistance. "No, thank you," I expressed my dissatisfaction. "I'm alright," I said, but I wasn't.

In the end, my date returned with me to my flat in a similar building... one step at a time.I sat on the sofa, trying to convince her (and myself) that I wasn't a complete jerk. I went to the kitchen, got the Tums, took a couple, and sat down again, still concerned that I might throw up and destroy everything.This is a bad idea. My fear of truly letting go again became a reality almost immediately. My companion remained in the other room, shocked, frequently asking, "Are you OK, babe?" I had hardly arrived to the latrine before vomiting vehemently into it.I was a shadow of the guy I had been a few of hours before when I finally emerged from the toilet, and I reluctantly agreed that she should phone 911.The paramedics arrived quickly, brought me out on a cot, and drove me to a neighboring medical clinic's trauma center, where attendants hooked me up to equipment and did a few tests.Two people died away in beds across the room as I lay there healing. I'm not joking when I say that I'm serious. They tucked them away and carted them away, just like on television.Finally, an expert appeared to pass on the results of my tests, but when I inquired about the outcome, all he could say was that I "had vertigo."Isn't that all? You dope, I'm sure I was dizzy. That seemed obvious to me.I needed to know why I felt dizzy and how to prevent it from happening again, but he had no idea, and neither did I when I was sent home.I'm going to spend the rest of my life worrying about my next assault and avoiding workouts that could set it off.The prospect of living like that enraged me for a variety of reasons, including the massive disaster for my confidence, beauty, and well-being, as well as the logical impact on my single male existence.I wasn't surprised when my yoga class date stopped responding my calls since high-quality single females weren't looking for someone who was barely holding on. She was the last person I ever saw.I'm guessing she saw a different angel. I'm not sure how this is happening to me.Was I supposed to just accept the presence of middle-aged mediocre quality without hesitation? There's no way in hell I'm going to do that.I'd take things into my own hands if the experts weren't going to provide me any useful advice or, at the very least, help me get my sh-t together.

Chapter Two

Answers in Search

The first thing I did was do a thorough examination of my eating habits.I knew from a long history of involvement with health and fitness, including a couple of years spent training alongside famous muscle heads, competitors, and entertainers at Gold's Gym in Venice, CA, that eating habits, not exercise, account for roughly 80% of success in losing weight and getting fit.Plus, if I attempted another round of P90X or another strenuous fitness program, my dizziness reappeared, but not to the same degree, and I was able to complete the workout quickly. When I wasn't working out, it tormented me sometimes as well. I'd be walking down the street when I lost my balance for no apparent reason, and I couldn't stop wondering what the fck was going on.By no means did I get the replies I was looking for right away.I looked at a variety of diets, including low-carb, high-carb, low-fat, squeezing, veggie-lovers, gluten-free, Mediterranean, and weight-loss programs. I also studied books and watched videos regarding the dangers of sugar from experts in the area including Dr. Richard Jacoby, Dr. Robert Lustig, Dave Zinczenko, Gary Taubes, and others.It took years and a lot of patience, but when I tried to figure out which diet (and accompanying exercise plan) was the most popular, I discovered something incredible: Despite a variety of drawbacks associated with the most well-known low-carb diets, including severe manageability concerns, the great majority of them functioned for the time being... Many of the great carb diets, though, did as well.This incredible revelation complicated and effectively postponed my decision on the best course of action, but it also raised a major dilemma...What is the difference between low-carb and high-carb diets?How is it even imaginable, especially given their proclivity to blame one another?

Chapter Three

What connects them?

Is there a way to take the finest of the distinctions and forget the rest? There is, in fact,When you cut through the hype and metaphor, you'll see that all successful weight-loss programs perform three things:Subtract sugar from the equation, add fiber, and subtract alcohol from the equation.Folks, there you have it: the Sugar Belly Secret.If you're really trying, you can increase your activity (and get more rest) by a factor of two for considerably better results. That is my primary concern, and I hope you will join me for some fundamental, tummy-tucking workouts in the future, but it is excessive.It is not mandatory to practice.The Sugar Belly Secret is not a "diet" in the traditional sense, yet that is precisely its beauty. People who consume less carbohydrates are often perplexed. Simply add and remove the following items: Subtract the excess sugar and liquor found in tampered, fraudulent, or deadly products from the fiber found in real, solid things.It's a tried-and-true way to lose weight, maintain and build fat-burning muscle, and improve your overall health and wellness without tracking calories, carbohydrates, or healthy fats, or even exercising. Pretty

Chapter Four

Isn't it simple?

It's not that quick.The sugar anteroom, staple, and café companies have sufficiently managed, repackaged, debased, contaminated (and, according to some experts, poisoned) our food supply to the point that it's extraordinarily impossible to avoid burning through fiberless food with added sugar and becoming obese.They've also stifled efforts by the FDA and others to increase transparency about the amount of added sugar in our food and beverages by delaying the implementation of a new nutrition label that would have allowed us to make better informed decisions as consumers by requiring companies to reveal the total"addedsugars"in their products.They need you out of the loop, and I'd rather not say it. Most firms aren't keen about relabeling their things, and it will cost a considerable amount of money to improve a major number of their items if buyers wise up and examine choices.Meanwhile, the US government has been unwilling to stir up controversy by mandating greater transparency, owing to a neurotic fear of losing political commitments and tax cash, and a few offices have acted as willing aids, whether intentionally or unintentionally.The partisan principle goes like this: If you get a sugar stomach, get sick, spend years in pain, or die young because you eat too much processed foods and drinks, it's your problem, not theirs. The vast majority of these businesses, organizations, and government institutions are unwilling to assist you in making better informed judgments.It's up to you to educate yourself, understand what's going on behind the scenes, and act.The costs of not doing so are not funny—indeed, they're dangerous—and they're growing with your girth at a rapid pace.According to a recent, in-depth study conducted by the University of Washington's Institute of Health Metrics and Evaluation, poor eating habits are now responsible for one out of every five deaths, with obesity being the fastest-growing global threat. Following smoking, diet is the second most significant risk factor for premature death.Similarly, according to a new research from the Centers for Disease Control and Prevention, 40 percent (40%) of all malignant growth analyses in the United States are presently linked to excess weight, with the majority (55%) of all tumors studied in women.This book was written to help you understand the sugar midsection disaster, get more fit, and stay strong by (a) spotting and removing sugar from a wide range of foods and beverages, much of which has been purposefully hidden from you; (b) spotting and adding fiber, much of which has been removed from food against your willpower; and (c) spotting and removing cocktails that are keeping you fat, debilitated, and troubled. It worked for me when I discovered the Sugar Belly Secret, and it continues to work for me now.Today, at the age of 55, I seem to be more grounded and more grounded than I was fourteen years ago following my first round of P90X, and I've had the opportunity to properly sustain my results over time.As I write this, I'm in my prime, living and working in Medellin, Colombia, surrounded by the most laid-back people you'll ever meet and, without a doubt, the most beautiful women on the planet.I'm also assisting others in getting in shape, staying healthy, and becoming fit —in person, on paper, on tape, and on the internet—and I'm certain that this book will spread the word to a far larger audience, starting with you.And, with God's help, my dizziness is no longer a problem. I'll never know what caused it or why it went away, but I do know that making the decision to remove my sugar gut and become healthy again was crucial.In any event, no one knows where I'd be. Not in a yoga class, for example.I'm not a doctor or a researcher, but I've spent my whole life immersed in health and wellness, have a remarkable story to tell as a P90X example of conquering hardship and casting part, and understand what it's like to self-destruct then come back. I really and sincerely came to my conclusions in this book after extensive and very personal inquiry.My life was in jeopardy, and I was desperate to reclaim it My sugar belly needed to be smoothed. Not some yo-yo nonsense, but I needed to look and feel amazing for the rest of my life. Additionally, this is what occurred.You, too, amigo, can accomplish it, no matter how obese, elderly, disabled, or dubious you are right now.You have the ability to defeat sugar in your belly and become the hero of your own narrative.You may either ignore or excuse the insights in this book, allowing the food and beverage industries, sugar campaigns, and degenerate lawmakers to mislead and manipulate you, and wasting your time on this planet playing with obesity, chronic illness, and premature death.(If you're going to do it, you may as well start smoking as well.)Best of luck if you're hoping to be rescued by a wise legislator or civil servant, a magic weight loss prescription, a trendy diet or fitness program, or well-informed food and beverage sector practices.It doesn't matter if they can't rescue you.You've got this, and I'd be honored to guide you in the right direction.The Sugar Belly Secret and the unvarnished facts about why it works better than anything else, starting with the straight scoop on sugar, are all you actually desire.

Chapter Five

Sugar

The LowdownI believed I had learned all there was to know about sugar. Was I mistaken, kid?It isn't to the point of avoiding pop, snacks, and candy entirely. It's no longer the case.Even limiting carbohydrates, which many people are aware turn to sugar in the body, is insufficient.The problem is far more serious, and the truth horrified me completely. I'm hoping it works for you as well.Every year, the average American consumes around 160 pounds of sugar, or more than 7 ounces per day, including 63 pounds of high-fructose corn syrup ("HFCS"), the most dangerous kind of added sugar known to induce instinctive (intra-organ) fat, which wasn't even accessible until 1975.That's before you factor in the use of alcoholic beverages.Imagine burning through 27 to 30 teaspoons of sugar per day to get a clearer picture.Would you eat that much sugar on purpose if you knew it was hurting, maybe damaging, and ultimately killing you as it grew your girth and multiplied your jaw? slowly, but steadily?I doubt it, especially after you've had your fill of extra sugar. If you want the unmistakable truth, you've come to the right place... As a result, I'm not going to exclude it.The Belly of "Additional Sugar"You've almost probably heard the story of America's stoutness epidemic by now, but you may be perplexed as to who the culprit is.It isn't fats that are causing the problem. Since roughly 1930, we've drastically reduced our fat consumption, but you wouldn't know it if you watched the news.Despite the claims of top-rated publications to the contrary, it's neither salt or gluten unless you have a specific problem with them.It's not carbohydrates in general since a lot of carbs don't make you fat or lethargic—quite the reverse, as several well-researched high-carb calorie counts have revealed.And it isn't you, regardless of if you've made a few haphazard diet and exercise decisions over time. Who hasn't done anything like that? I'm not advocating for an exploitative mindset since blaming others is a recipe for inactivity and complacency, even in the face of failure, and each of us has a great deal of responsibility for our actions.But, after decades of being spoon-fed phony food and bogus news about it, it's difficult to make educated consumer judgments.So, in this tale, who is the true rogue? Handled or sugared, you've got it.You don't only get a sugar belly when you eat carbohydrates with excessive amounts of added sugar, such as sucrose, fructose, and HFCS, which may be found in sodas, organic drink beverages, snacks, and other food sources.You throw your digestion into a downward spiral, resulting in a set of increasingly normal disorders known as metabolic disorder, which include obesity, type 2 diabetes, cholesterol difficulties, hypertension, and cardiovascular infection, all of which lead to inevitable misery and premature death.I don't disagree with certain experts who claim that prolonged exposure to added sugar causes cancer, Alzheimer's, IBS, and other horrible things.From 1822 to 2005, here's a graph of sugar consumption in the United States:Sugar consumption averages 120 pounds per person per year, which was high enough to pass on all of the data back in 2005, but according to some estimates, we're up to approximately 160 pounds per person per year in 2017. Assume the chart looks like this now. Although there have been a few unintentional dunks in the direction in recent years, the vertical trend has mostly continued.Examine the following graph, which shows adult stoutness rates in the United States from 1990 to 2016, with one line for each of the 50 states:Do the patterns of sugar consumption and obesity strike you as odd? It's no surprise that the rate and prevalence of obesity have risen in tandem with the amount of sugar consumed in the United States.When these state-by-state figures were updated on August 31, 2017, adult obesity rates exceeded 35% in five states (with West Virginia leading the pack at 37.7%), 30% in 25 states, and 25% in 46 states (with Colorado raising the back, maybe, at 22.3 percent).Pound-for-pound, what does it imply?We're around 25% heavier than we were 25 years ago, and the evidence of our collective tubbiness isn't hard to find.Only around 15% of adults in the United States were overweight or obese in 1980. As a result, normal weight people are no longer the norm, and the proportion of overweight and stout adults in the US is expected to rise to 65 percent by 2030.Although the majority of Americans now have a sugar stomach, don't think you're unaffected if you don't. According to studies, up to 40% of average-weight adults suffer from "insulin blockage," a sign of chronic metabolic disease. So, what exactly is it? It's a ticking time bomb waiting to explode on a slew of naive people who believe they're solid just because they're not as obese as their neighbor.All things considered, obesity is no longer only a Western or American problem. It's an epidemic that has spread over the planet.I take delight in seeing Coca-Cola, McDonald's, KFC, and other American companies advertised in large metropolitan centers across the former Soviet Union, but as we've poisoned our food supply by adding massive amounts of sugar (and reducing fiber), we've offered our children a sugar-free diet.Our obesity is also a problem for the rest of the globe.Another study published in the prestigious New England Journal of Medicine found that 2.2

billion people (or 33% of the global population, with the United States leading the way) are overweight or obese right now.How did so many people from all over the world, who had previously been delicate or average weight, end up joining the sugartummy club?They consumed a lot more processed food and beverages from the West, which are obviously tasty and reasonably priced, but are typically heavy in sugar and poor in fiber.Up the FructusIsn't all sugar the same?No, it's not true, and understanding the difference is crucial. Carbohydrates are made up of three different types of sugar:Glucose (glucose) is a kind of sugar that isSucrose (table sugar) is a kind of sugar that is found in a variety of foods.

Fructose is the third sugar (regularly in the fluid type of HFCS).Sucrose is a combination of glucose and fructose that is half glucose and half fructose. HFCS, on the other hand, contains up to 55 percent fructose, tastes better, costs less, and comes in a liquid form.Every cell in your body can process glucose (also known as "life energy"), increasing the capacity and likelihood of consuming it. However, fructose can only be metabolized by your liver, which filters toxins (including alcohol), and chronic fructose exposure causes metabolic syndrome and other serious health issues.Although fructose is a carb, it is used by your body as a fat. That is, when your liver reacts to fructose, it floods your body with fatty substances (greasy stores in your blood), telling your body to store more tummy fat, which is exactly what happens.At the end of the day, you're consuming fat when you burn through fructose. For your waistline, it's the worst kind of sugar.In one experiment, participants drank beverages containing either glucose or fructose for an extended period of time. They gained roughly the same amount of weight by the end of the study, but those who consumed fructose gained weight primarily as sugar-gut fat due to the way the liver processes the sugar.Sucrose and HFCS are both harmful because they transport fructose to your liver and expand your sugar midsection, but HFCS is particularly problematic because of its fluid structure, added taste, and lower cost, which makes it a financial incentive for companies to secretly add it to soda pops, bread, prepared foods, tidbits, sauce, and... you name it.We used to get our fructose from fruits and vegetables before food processing, but it wasn't much, and those foods are high in fiber and micronutrients, so the trade-off was worth it.offworthwhile... the past and the presentHowever, as adults, teenagers, and children, fructose now accounts for an irrationally large percentage of the calories we consume in food and beverages. It's astronomically high.

Chapter Six

There must be a sacrifice made

MisinformationThere's a lot of false information and misrepresentation about food out there, but the most egregious kind has to do with low-fat diets (which divert attention away from fructose and other added sugars), the phrase "a calorie is a calorie," and marketing campaigns aimed at making obesity appealing.Diets that are low in fat are ineffective.The US government and some ostensibly nutritional experts have been recommending low-fat weight-loss plans for more than 35 years, claiming that they reduce "awful" cholesterol while also preventing obesity and heart disease.Regrettably, they based their decisions on flawed investigations, including Ancel Keys' influential 500-page "Seven Countries" report from 1980.Mr. Keys accepted and attempted to demonstrate that dietary fat was the sole cause of coronary artery disease because of its cholesterol content.

Regardless, as Dr. Robert Lustig and other sugar experts have pointed out, Keys failed to recognize that he was focusing on the effects of high-fructose diets, not high-fat diets, because fructose is processed similarly to fat. He also failed to distinguish between two types of low-density lipoproteins (LDL). Huge amounts of low-density lipoprotein (LDL) are not harmful; however, small amounts of high-density lipoprotein (HDL) are.We understand that now, but back then, the food industry responded to the US government's low-fat rules by offering a diverse range of low-fat food options. Consider what they did, given that low-fat food has the same aftertaste as Styrofoam. To make it more appealing, they added sugar, and our consumption of sugar and weight increased dramatically.Low-fat diets have been a colossal failure since then. They've increased obesity, sickness, and death by allowing the contamination of our food supply with processed sugar, and they're not done yet because people continue to sell and believe false information about them.To put it another way, if you prefer or require a larger sugar stomach, stick to a low-fat diet. In any case, consign them to history's trash heap.There Are Some Calories That Are Better Than OthersIf "a calorie is a calorie," as some argue, it is up to you to either burn or store the calories you consume through food or drink. If you eat too much or too little, this mantra saysYou will gain weight if you exercise to the point of exhaustion.I'm sure you've heard this well-known concept repeated by food and beverage companies (which would rather not improve their products), insurance companies (which need a reason to deny coverage), doctors (who are frequently under-prepared in terms of nutrition), recreation centers (which rely on people not showing up), weight loss centers (which need you as a customer), and other businesses selling exercise programs and supplements.Many of these calorie counters believe that if you're unhappy with your results from whatever they're offering, they can blame you by claiming that you burned too many calories, didn't exercise enough to burn them off, or both. But it's not as simple as that, because the quality of your calories is just as important as the quantity.Calories from solid complex carbs, proteins, and fats contribute to overall health, longevity, and a flat stomach. Calories from added sugars, fiberless foods, and most alcoholic beverages contribute to weight gain, metabolic disease, and other health problems.The distinction could not be clearer, but we're still burning through a lot of calories from some questionable sources, thanks to caloric relativism to some extent. That has to change, and now is not the time to squander an ideal opportunity. Counting calories isn't necessary. The Sugar Belly Secret will help you maximize your calorie intake.Obesity is neither attractive nor desirable, so please accept my apologies.Obesity isn't just unattractive to the other gender. It's unappealing, and it could be fatal.Do you want to know if someone will die young? Look at how slim they are.(After that, observe their walking patterns.) They don't have that many years left, assuming they walk slowly. As a result, put the pie down and get a move on!)Despite these facts, the media and the fashion industry frequently attempt to rethink what it means to be ordinary, genuine, cool, lovely, healthy, or even "advanced" by promoting overweight women and, to a lesser extent, men.

Chapter Seven

The other option

The other option, which is to see the obvious or to simply express current realities, amounts to "fat shaming."With all due respect, I don't have the patience for this level of arousal, and I don't think it's healthy for you either. It's completely false, and those who believe it harm themselves by encouraging them to stay fat, ugly, and, most importantly, unhealthy.All I care about is helping you look better, feel better, and live longer by taking a sugar-paunch step forward, and publicity like this helps us back down.We don't have the stamina to play word games or flag pictures. There's a lot of work ahead of us.Rejoice!Are you sticking to your sugar gut no matter what? Regardless of how it feels right now, there isn't a chance.It's never too late to get rid of your sugar belly, and it's much easier than you might think.This book will show you how by revealing the real problem and presenting a simple solution, beginning with a description of the Hormone Game that is playing out inside each of us.Your body will handle the rest, and your sugar gut will be a thing of the past if you play the Game brilliantly by removing the agitators (sugar and liquor) and adding an underappreciated peacemaker (fiber).It's possible that you'll lose a couple of larger-budget demonstrating gigs, but that's probably for the best.

Chapter Eight

Hormones

Hormones at WarI went from P9oX Joe to Average Joe after losing a Hormone Game ("Game") that I didn't realize I was playing.But the show doesn't end until the fat lady sings.I got rid of my sugar gut for good once I figured out how to play the Game. You can, too, but dominating a game you're unfamiliar with is difficult.This section will explain everything in layman's terms, starting with this crucial point: The game's main goal is to lower your insulin level.That's right, since we need to consume energy and fat rather than store it, everything revolves around insulin, also known as the energy- or fat-stockpiling chemical.You lose the Match and gain control of an unappealing, unfortunate sugar gut if you raise your insulin level. If you do the opposite, you'll win the game, slim down your midsection, and transform your life. Those are the two main options available to you.Remember that as we look at leptin, insulin, ghrelin, dopamine, and cortisol, five of the most important chemicals in the game.Leptin (also known as "satiety hormone") is a hormone that helps people feel satisfied.Leptin is a chemical produced by fat cells that tells your brain when you've stored enough energy as fat, and it also tells you when you've spent too much time doing so.When it's working properly, leptin will prevent you from overeating.When your cerebrum does not receive the leptin signal as it should, things get out of hand. It switches to starvation mode and instructs the rest of your body to figure out what's wrong by reducing your energy consumption (i.e., draining you) and increasing your hunger (i.e., causing you to eat more).Leptin isn't working as well as it used to, and that's the problem with it. Leptin resistance is a term for something that isn't quite right.Imagine leptin trying to signal to your brain that you're ready to eat some fat after a big meal, but something gets in the way, making your brain think you really want another serving or, even worse, dessert.It's a pulverizing internal correspondence problem.Almost every one of the world's 2.2 billion overweight and corpulent people suffers from leptin obstruction, and they won't be able to lose their sugar stomachs for any significant period of time unless and until this hidden problem is addressed.So, what's causing the leptin signal in your cerebrum to be in opposition? There's a lot of insulin in this game. What's the source of the insulin overabundance? Overuse of sugar, you guessed it.Insulin (also known as "fat storage hormone") is a hormone that regulates the storage of fat in the body.Insulin is a hormone produced by your pancreas that allows your body to block the action of leptin and store energy as fat for later use (weight gain).Insulin causes sugar-midsection fat to form as a result of this.Your body stores more energy as fat when your insulin levels rise.The converse occurs when it falls. You lose weight and your fat cells therapist.When your body is working as an even, fat-burning machine, this recurring pattern is as smooth as silk. There are times when you need to burn calories without insulin and other times when you need to store them as fat. Under certain circumstances, storing energy as fat is a good thing.However, if you have too much insulin in your system (hyperinsulinemia), leptin won't tell your brain to burn calories even if you're already full. As previously stated, your brain interprets (or misinterprets) this as a sign of hunger, instructing your body to (a) store more energy as fat by increasing your appetite while decreasing your physical activity, and (b) release a lot more insulin!Furthermore, when your insulin level is too high for an extended period of time and your fat, muscle, and liver cells can no longer withstand the attack, your body begins to reject or oppose the insulin completely, causing a new set of problems in the Game.Insulin resistance is not to be confused with leptin obstruction, despite the fact that both are harmful to your health. When this occurs in the liver, the excess sugar is converted to "liver fat," which causes the pancreas to produce significantly more insulin, resulting in significantly more energy being stored as body fat.Finally, the excess insulin caused by leptin resistance and insulin resistance expands your sugar midsection by ensuring constant energy storage as fat and the weight gain that comes with it. It's a never-ending cycle that's also a common obesity formula.Our insulin levels are two to multiple times higher today than they were 40 years ago, causing leptin flagging, causing leptin and insulin opposition, and turning us into a sugar guts country, with the rest of the world not far behind.Leptin Signaling Enhancement and Insulin ReductionWhat would you do if you had to break the cycle and turn the game around?With the Sugar Belly Secret, you can lower your insulin levels and improve leptin motion, which is why stage one includes eliminating sugar from your diet, especially sucrose (glucose and fructose) and HFCS.Many of the best low-carb diets recommend limiting your intake of sugar and other (generally refined or processed) foods high in starches, which your body converts to sugar (glucose). If your body can't use glucose for energy because you didn't eat a lot of carbohydrates, it will turn to fat for energy, which is what happens most of the time.These weight-loss plans may work in the short term because the wide net cast over all carbs catches added sugars as well as nearly everything else, but many people can't or don't want to eat this way for long periods of time. In the event that they are not carried out properly, medical conditions such as nutrient deficiencies may arise.I tried the Ketogenic diet once and lost some weight, but it left me exhausted, frail, and unusually drained. It forced me to give up some of my favorite non-sweet or potentially high-fiber foods, and I'm almost certain I've caught a bug since I stopped eating natural product to reduce my daily carb intake.I have no intention of criticizing the Ketogenic diet. It works if you stick with it, and it's good for quick weight loss. It also includes some sugar-busting stomach hacks (such as intermittent fasting), but I can't stick to that diet for more than a few days or weeks without cheating. It's just not something I'm interested in.And here's the best part: if your carbs are low in sugar and high in fiber, you don't need to cut them out entirely.For example, a whole organic product contains sugar, but it also contains fiber, which slows carb assimilation and glucose retention in the circulatory system, relieves liver heat, and lowers insulin response. It's also packed with vitamins, minerals, and micronutrients.The Sugar Belly Secret recommends incorporating fiber into your diet for this reason.There's no compelling reason to eat a lot of carbs, with or without sugar, as long as there's enough fiber to balance things out and keep your insulin from destroying the game.Ghrelin (also known as "hunger hormone") is a hormone that causes people to feel hungry.While you're reducing leptin resistance and insulin resistance with the Sugar Belly Secret, there's another hormone you can and should reduce: gherelin, also known as the "hunger hormone."While the Sugar Belly Secret does not recommend calorie counting or obsessing over segment sizes, gorging is never a good idea, especially when trying to lose weight.What methods would you use to reduce ghrelin levels?To begin, make certain you're getting enough protein in your diet. High-protein dinners lower ghrelin levels faster than high-carb or high-fat dinners, according to studies. Protein-rich dinners also cause a more sensitive insulin response than low-carb meals, and everything revolves around lowering insulin levels.Second, get more rest because when you're sleep deprived, ghrelin levels rise. When I don't get enough rest, which happens more often than I'd like to admit, I've seen this. I assumed I ate more when I was restless because my body needed the extra energy (and a lot of espresso) to wake up, but it's more complicated than that.Although it's a hormonal issue, we can reduce our ghrelin levels (and thus our hunger) by eating more protein-rich dinners and getting plenty of sleep. Easy as pie.Dopamine (the "pleasure" neurohormone) is a neurohormone that helps people feel good about themselves.Dopamine is a neurohormone or synapse that regulates reward and pleasure centers in the brain.According to New York University scientists, when insulin spikes (after a delicious dinner), it triggers the release of dopamine because we love to eat—especially if the food or refreshment is syrupy—and dopamine generally lasts as long as the insulin.If you're overweight, however, dopamine doesn't work the same way.Larger people get a similar dopamine boost when they see food, but they don't get a similar "reward" signal when they eat it, according to studies. It's just not as enjoyable as they expected, most likely due to the insulin obstructing this reaction, making them compelled to return for another nibble... in search of that elusive reward.I'm not sure why this happens, but I'm aware that repeating the same behavior too frequently can result in desensitization. It won't be long before it's no longer remarkable. Soon, we'll either want more of it to get a similar "high," or we'll lose interest entirely.Fat people are similar to drug addicts in this regard. They keep coming back for more candy coated stuff because they can't seem to get to the point where they feel as good as they used to, and the prize for doing so becomes increasingly difficult to achieve over time.That's a sad story about a happy chemical, but there's another chemical—ostensibly the most important in your body—that you'd like to acquire, respect, and master in order to dominate the Hormone Match.Cortisol (also known as "stress hormone") is a hormone that is produced in response to a stressful situation.Without cortisol, the stress chemical, we can't deal with any stress in our lives. Regardless,Isn't it true that no one wants a lot of stress?

Without a doubt, no.I've long believed that high levels of stress accelerate the aging, debilitation, and death of individuals, and it turns out that I was correct.Excessive exposure to cortisol from stress over time causes your body to produce sugar-stomach fat, which is linked to metabolic disorders and leads to insulin resistance, lack of sleep, and the use of filling "soothing foods."

Chapter Nine

What options are available to you?

Plenty.MeditateMany health and wellness experts recommend contemplation to help you reduce cortisol, center your mind, and live in the moment.Let it all out if that's your thing, because it works.Years ago, I practiced reflection and now see how beneficial it was. I'm also aware that a significant number of the world's most accomplished people practice it in some way.So, after a long break, I'm giving it another shot right now, thanks to a friend who told me about Headspace. If you're interested, take a look at it.Meditation is cool and sound, but for the past 15 years, it hasn't been a big part of my stress-reduction routine.Sleep and exercise are two of the things that help me lower my cortisol levels.It's Time To SleepSleep deprivation disrupts your Game by raising cortisol levels, decreasing leptin levels, and raising insulin levels, all of which increase your chances of developing sugar stomach and obesity.Oh, and it's possible that it's also killing you.Professor Matthew Walker, director of the University of California, Berkeley's Center for Human Sleep Science, claims that a "devastating sleep loss pestilence" is affecting every aspect of our biology and causing potentially fatal illnesses and conditions such as diabetes, obesity, coronary disease, Alzheimer's, stroke, and cancer.I don't know what else to say if that isn't reason enough to get more Z's. What could be easier than taking more time to relax?Please accept my heartfelt gratitude.

Chapter Ten

Big Guy, take a walk

Although it is possible to reduce cortisol without exercising, there may be no better way.Any form of exercise will not reduce your anxiety quickly, effectively, or affordably. It reduces insulin resistance while simultaneously consuming stubborn muscle and instinctive (sugar gut) fat.You've probably heard that physical activity increases cortisol (stress) levels while you're doing it. While this is true, it also lowers your cortisol levels for the rest of the day.Overall, the time and effort invested are well worth it.Plus, combining exercise with the Sugar Belly Secret will improve your appearance, particularly if you want to add muscle to your slimmer waistline.Now that my vertigo is gone, I exercise on a regular basis, which I enjoy.I always feel great afterwards and meet new friends with similar interests, in addition to improving my appearance, health, and fitness. In the middle of a workout, I also have a tendency to have some of my best ideas. (It happens in the shower as well, but that's beside the point.)Winning!The Sugar Belly Secret will help you win the Game of Hormones by improving your leptin signaling, lowering your ghrelin, maintaining proper dopamine function, lowering cortisol, and, most importantly, lowering your insulin level (and burning more fat)!That's how sugar belly loss works biologically.Let's begin by eliminating sugar from our diet. In Chapter 3, you'll learn how to do it step-by-step.

Chapter Eleven

Sugar should be removed.

When I first started doing P90 in my home office in Miami Beach, FL in November 2001, I'd take coffee breaks by walking a few blocks to Starbucks for a large ("Venti") Caffé Mocha.I only drank one a day on occasion, but I drank two on the majority of days.I loved my Mochas and thought of them as a reward for all my hard work, but after a while, I couldn't help but notice something in the mirror. My belly was expanding despite my P90 workouts, low-stress lifestyle, and (I thought) relatively healthy diet.I didn't know why I was gaining weight.I eventually solved the mystery by using a process of elimination (removing a specific food or beverage from my diet for a period of time to see if it made a difference).Starbucks Caffé Mochas were the culprit.This discovery did not sit well with me, and I did not immediately go cold turkey.I limited myself to one per day, but it was enough of a difference to notice. Almost immediately, my waist began to shrink.I lost all of the extra weight I had been carrying after completely replacing mochas with regular coffee.I couldn't believe it, to tell you the truth. Removing chocolate-flavored coffee from my diet was a relatively minor change that paid off big time.I'm not sure what it was about those Caffé Mochas that made me so fat. On its website, Starbucks answers the question.A 20-ounce venti Caffé Mocha with whole milk and no whipped cream has 53 grams of carbohydrates, 43 of which are sugar.If I had added whipped cream (which I didn't, but could have), the sugar content would have increased to 45 grams, along with some unhealthy trans fat for good measure.Isn't that awful?A 12 gram glazed donut from Dunkin' Donuts has less sugar than one of my Starbucks Caffé Mochas by more than 3 12 times. (To be fair, other Dunkin' Donuts menu items spit sand in the face of Starbucks Caffé Mochas on sugar belly beach.) For example, if you order a large Vanilla Bean Coolatta from Dunkin' Donuts with your glazed donut, you'll add another 174 grams of sugar to your total sugar rush, bringing it to a sickening 186 grams.)A Pepsi would be nice. A 20-ounce bottle of Pepsi has 69 grams of sugar, according to PepsiCo's own website.A 20-ounce bottle of Coke, on the other hand, has 65 grams of sugar in it.My 20-oz. Starbucks Caffé Mochas weren't quite as bad as a Pepsi or Coke of comparable size, but they were close, and as previously stated, I usually drank more than one. When I drank two mochas per day, I was consuming 86 grams of sugar, and that's before I factored in whatever junk I was eating with my coffee at the time.To give you an idea of how much sugar is in two Caffé Mochas, the WHO recommends no more than 25 grams of sugar per day. Although some government agencies in the United States allow for a higher number of grams, the bottom line is that the less added sugar you consume, the better, and these drinks will easily exceed your daily sugar quota.

Back in 2001, I had a problem with an unexplainably bloated sugar belly, but I figured out what was causing it, cut off the sugar, dropped weight, and never looked back.Since then, more than 15 years have gone, and I've made lots of dietary blunders, but one of them isn't consuming Starbucks Caffé Mochas.I've never had another one, and I'm not sure I miss them. It's the end of that.My Achilles' heel was Caffé Mochas. Which one is it for you?It's likely that there are many foods or drinks involved, but that's OK.You may get rid of your sugar belly by detecting and removing sugar from the foods and beverages you eat, and the remainder of this chapter will guide you through the process, beginning with the most obvious culprits, sugar bombs.Sugar Bombs must be dropped.Do I really need to urge you to cut down on candy, cookies, cake, drink, ice cream, doughnuts, and other sugary treats? Probably not, but have a look at the stunning images from the event below.Sugar cubes and blocks, as used by SinAzucar.org, are a universal metaphor.I'm not picking on Starbucks since I like the atmosphere of their cafés, and they're not alone in putting so much sugar in their drinks, but Starbucks' venti Frappuccino is a sugar bomb.It has 76 grams of sugar in it, which is equal to 19 sugar cubes. That's revolting, people. It should be discarded.As an alternative, how about Cappuccino? I mean, what's the harm?While certain Cappuccinos are lower in sugar than others, if you're not paying attention, you're still playing with fire.Take, for example, the Nescafe Cappuccino. Sugar accounts for over half of it.Instead, make a cup of ordinary coffee.While you're at it, leave out the Minute Maid fruit juice.Minute Maid Peach ("Melocoton" in Spanish) juice has 42.9 grams of sugar in a 300 milliliter (10.14 ounce) container. This isn't good for your stomach.Nutella is another option.It's tasty—I tasted it in Germany a couple times—but it's 56.8% sugar!You're done with Nutella.What about Ben & Jerry's, the "progressive" ice cream duo?Surely, dumping gobs of sugar on people wouldn't make them obese and sick?Wrong. Ben & Jerry's Chunky Monkey ice cream comes in a relatively tiny 250 mL container.15 sugar cubes in 60 grams of sugarYou'd be in luck if it was a stack of poker chips, but it isn't, and you aren't. Regardless of your political stance, you need always be cautious when buying anything.Energy drinks, such as Red Bull, are the same way. I used to drink them by the bottle and as a mixer in my alcoholic beverages.Red Bull has 52 grams of sugar in a 16-ounce bottle.Red Bull may not give you wings, but it will give you a sugar belly. If you aren't cautious, so will ketchup.Heinz Ketchup, for example, has 12 grams of sugar per 55 grams of product.After reading about massive sugar bombs like Red Bull and Nutella, it may not seem that horrible, but adding that much ketchup to your meal is like adding a glazed doughnut from Dunkin Donuts.Will using Heinz Curry Mango Sauce instead of Heinz Ketchup fix the issue? Nope. There's 39 grams of sugar in a bottle of that stuff. Other sugar bombs to eliminate right away from your diet are:Vitaminwater Focus, Mrs. Butterworth's Original Syrup (47 g sugar), Mrs. Butterworth's Original Syrup (47 g sugar), Mrs. Butterworth's Original SyrKiwi Strawberry (32 grams of sugar), Ocean Spray Cran-Apple (31 grams of sugar), Tazo Organic Iced Green Tea (30 grams of sugar), PowerBar Cookie Dough (29 grams of sugar), Quaker Natural Granola Apple Cranberry Almond (27 grams of sugar), Kashi GoLean Snacks Granola Bar (27 grams of sugar), Dannon All-Natural Lowfat Yogurt (27 grams of sugar), Dannon All-Natural Lowfat Yogurt (27 gramsNature Valley Oats & Honey Granola Bars (25 grams sugar), KIND Almonds and Apricots Yogurt Bar (16 grams sugar), Bertolli Tomato and Basil (12 grams sugar), and Lemon (11 grams of sugar).I could go on, but I'm sure you get the idea, right?SugarspottingAfter you've eliminated the sugar bombs (save for special occasions and the odd treat), it's time to identify and eliminate sugary foods and drinks that aren't as obvious.You can accomplish it, even though it's difficult at times.I wish I could tell you that all you have to do is look at the added sugars data on products with a Nutrition Facts label, but you won't find it on most products because the sugar lobby successfully lobbied the US government to postpone compliance with a rule that would have required it indefinitely.The Food and Drug Administration (FDA) authorized a new Nutrition Facts label with a distinct line for "Added Sugars" in May of 2016, which, if adopted and enforced, will oblige food and beverage producers to differentiate between natural and added sugars for the first time.In my opinion, it was a wise action made for the correct reasons. They added a new line to "increase consumer awareness of the quantity of added sugars in foods" (my italics), based on recommendations for reduced added sugar consumption from organizations that really stepped up, such as the American Heart Association, American Academy of Pediatrics, Institute of Medicine, and World Health Organization.

Chapter Twelve

Here's how the old and new labels compare

:As you can see, the new label features a bigger, more accurate "Serving size" and "Servings per container" description, but the greatest part is the new "Added Sugars" information.The new label would make sugarspotting a lot simpler at a time when a lot of people are in need.Most of the time, however there are some flaws.Most crucially, by defining Added Sugars to exclude "fruit and vegetable juice condensed from 100 percent fruit juice... as well as certain sugars contained in fruit and vegetable juices, jellies, jams, preserves, and fruit spreads," the FDA created a "juice" loophole. Although juice has no added sugar, many top experts contend that the sugar in juice equivalent to additional sugar after the fiber from the fruit and vegetables is removed during processing, and I believe them.How did the FDA's new Nutrition Facts label end up in the trash?The

FDA set a July 26, 2018 deadline for firms with annual food sales of less than $10 million when it announced its new regulation in May of 2016. Manufacturers with annual food sales of less than $10 million were given an additional year to comply.Allowing firms enough time to modify their labels seemed sensible, but it also provided a window for the sugar lobby to exert pressure on government officials to delay or torpedo the whole process, which they did.The FDA announced its plan to extend the compliance deadlines... indefinitely on June 13, 2017 after "business and consumer organizations approached the FDA with comments about the compliance dates."Boom.For one reason or another, certain significant food and beverage corporations altered their Nutrition Facts labels. Nabisco/Mondelez used the labels on Wheat Thins crackers, KIND used them on granola bars, and PepsiCo used them on Lay's chips, Fritos, and Cheetos.Others took advantage of the "juice" loophole in the new Nutrition Facts label to make their products appear healthier than they are. Those companies deserve credit for being responsible and making our sugarspotting easier, but others took advantage of the "juice" loophole in the new Nutrition Facts label to make their products appear healthier than they are.For example, Naked Juice, Inc., a juice and smoothie company located in California, changed their label to include "Incl. 0g Added Sugars" beneath "Total Sugars 53g." This kind of deceitful labeling should not be trusted. If natural sugar from juice is just as harmful as added sugar since the fiber from the fruits and vegetables is removed during processing, then this is simply a cunning ploy to make this product seem healthy, get you to drink it, and then make you fat.Years ago, when I was growing soft and overweight, I used to frequently consume Naked Juice's "Green Machine." It tastes excellent and seems to be healthy at first appearance, but I never knew it had 53 grams of sugar in it or didn't care to check, and I didn't realize the necessity of fiber at the time.Well, I no longer make that error, and I doubt I'll ever drink another bottle.spending the rest of my life on Naked Juice Instead, I eat full, unprocessed fruits and veggies, and you should, too.Fortunately, perhaps because so many multinational corporations voluntarily adopted the new Nutrition Facts label, or perhaps because of pressure from consumers who began expecting to see it on new products and insisted that manufacturers admit it, or perhaps just government officials, many multinational corporations have voluntarily adopted the new Nutrition Facts label.The FDA has finally set a new deadline because they recognized they could no longer justify an indefinite delay in the new labeling standards.The FDA said on September 29, 2017 that major businesses would have until January 1, 2020 to comply with the new standards and begin printing the new Nutrition Facts labels on all processed and packaged goods. Smaller businesses have until January 1, 2021 to make the same modifications.That's excellent, if not terrific, news (better late than never), but your sugar belly, health, and fitness, as well as mine, can't wait until the next decade to start making wiser, more educated purchasing selections.We must begin to fight back by using the nutritional knowledge and tools that we have today, and we have a lot of them.Aside from paying attention to the "Total Sugars" data on current Nutrition Facts labels—if a product's Total Sugars are high, don't buy it—keep a watch on ingredient lists since food and beverage corporations use them to sneakily add sugar by renaming it something else.Alternative names for processed or added sugar include the following, which you should learn to recognize on ingredient labels:• Agave nectar (juice), nectar (nectar), sap (syrup), and syrup

Chapter Thirteen

Drisweet

• Barbados sugarSweetener made from dried raisin• Brown (sugar/rice syrup) • Buttered syrup • Cane (juice/sugar/syrup/crystals) • Evaporated cane • Blackstrap molassesCarob (syrup/powder) • Caramel• Castor sugar (also known as Berry sugar) • Chinese Rock Sugar • Clintose • Confectioner's (powdered) sugar• Fructose • Flomalt (sweetener)• Glazed and icing sugar • Fruit juice (concentrate)• Glaze icing sugar • Golden (sugar/syrup) • Gomme • Grape (sugar/syrup)• Icing sugar • Honiflake (aka Trimoline)• Lactose • Liquid sweetener • Malt • Maltose • Isoglucose • Isomaltulose • Kona ame• Organic raw sugar • Maple (sugar/syrup) • Mizu ame • Molasses • Muscovado sugarPanoche • Powdered sugar • Raw sugar • Demerara sugar • Dextrose • Granulated sugar • Panella (aka Rapadura)• Honibake • Refined sugar • High-fructose corn syrup• Ric e syrup • Rock sugar • Sorghum (syrup) • Starch sweetener • Sucanat • Sucrose • Sucrovert • Sugar beet • Sugar invert • Sweet n neat • Table sugar • Treacle • Trehalose • Tru sweet • Turbinado sugar • Vanilla sugar • VersatoseWhen food and beverage corporations attempt to pull a quick one on you, the more acquainted you are with these sugar code names, the more likely you will avoid items that contain them.Add, Add, Add, Add, Add, Add, Add, Add, Add, Add, Add, Add, Add, Add, AddAccording to a recent research, the following are the primary sugar sources in the American diet: Beverages containing sugar (37.1 percent),Cakes, cookies, and doughnuts (13.7%), fruit juice drinks (8.9%), dairy desserts including ice cream (6.1%), and candy (5.8 percent).It's your goal to eliminate as much of this as possible from your diet. What is the most efficient method of doing this?Take heed.Except for water and milk, subtract all beverages.Start by throwing out any sugary drinks you've previously bought, such as soda, juice, energy drinks, and vitamin water.Lactose, a relatively innocuous and not especially sweet sugar that your body converts to glucose rather than fructose, as well as numerous vital vitamins and minerals, are all found in unsweetened milk.Everything else, on the other hand, has to be removed.Fruit juice contains more sugar per cup than soda, thus it's included. So, instead of drinking your fruit, eat it whole and fiber-free.Only water and milk should be left after you've finished washing, although unsweetened coffee and tea are good as well. (I nearly always have a couple of cups of black coffee.)If you must, you may drink sugar-free sodas and other sugar-free or "light" items in moderation as a substitute for sugary ones—I cheat with Stevia in some of my snack foods, for example—but you're better off avoiding them altogether for three reasons.To begin with, sugar-free, low-calorie, and other "diet" beverages and snacks, according to a Yale University study published in August 2017, deceive your brain into making you bigger. This happens because your brain equates the taste of sugar with an influx of sugar and energy, and responds by instructing your pancreas to produce more insulin, which causes you to gain weight.Scientists aren't sure what happens when your brain recognizes the sugar and energy didn't come on time, but many feel this ruse in the Game of Hormones prompts you to seek sweets elsewhere, which leads to issues."A calorie is not a calorie," said Professor Dana Small, the study's lead author. "When sweet taste and energy [from sugar and carb calories] are not matched, less energy is digested, and erroneous signals are sent to the brain," says the study. Both of these things might have an impact on your metabolic health."Artificial sweeteners, too, create sugar belly, and this fact is clearly connected to the first. Increased use of diet sodas was linked to abdominal obesity in a 2015 research published in the Journal of the American Geriatrics Society. Approximately a nine-year period, older persons who used diet soda on a regular basis saw their waist circumference expand by over 3X more than those who did not.Third, the effects of all of these new artificial sweeteners on your health and fitness are still being determined.over a lengthy period of time Who knows what they're up to in their private lives? It's a guessing game. Why take the risk in light of all of this?Most sugar-free foods taste like chemicals anyhow, and after a time, you won't miss it. You could even discover that after you quit consuming diet sodas and drinks, you lose all desire for them and wonder why you ever did.Foods that fail the test are removed.Do you have any doughnuts, cake, or cookies?Unsuccessful reader That's all garbage.Please, right now, move it there and give yourself credit for doing so.Then repeat with any other item that fails the sugar-belly test in your refrigerator and cabinets.A food product must possess the following to pass the sugar-belly test:1. Little or no added sugar, with the caveat that you don't have to throw away every food product that has some added sugar (this is unrealistic and unsustainable), but you should use your judgment. Toss it if the extra sugar grams outnumber the fiber grams.3. No trans fats or Omega-6 fats, and at least 3 grams of fiber.Warning: While most "fats" are healthy and tasty (I love my avocado and almonds, for example), goods that contain processed trans fat or Omega-6 fats should be permanently deleted from your shopping list.You're probably doing it correctly if you need a larger garbage can after this subtraction exercise. Everything that doesn't pass the test has to be discarded.Don't worry about all that extra room in your refrigerator and kitchen cupboards. A vacuum is something that Mother Nature despises. You'll be purchasing actual, wholesome food to eat at home before you realize it, and your sugar belly will leave with it.Use Your Imagination When Eating OutI'm a bachelor who doesn't cook or have a lot of food or drinks in his apartment. I don't like cooking for one and tend to overeat if food is available when I'm at home working.That means I eat out at least once a day, and I've grown really good at it.When I go to a new restaurant and am unfamiliar with the menu, I make a few mistakes, but I've learned to order food and beverages that are low in added sugar and high in fiber the majority of the time, and I eat quite well.Restaurant food may be difficult to understand since it is sometimes delivered with little or no nutritional information. It may seem to be delicious on the menu, but looks may be misleading.To illustrate the issue, below are some statistics on added sugar in dishes from some of America's most prominent restaurants, all of which can be found simply online:Applebee's:Chicken Salad with Pecans (65 grams of sugar)Honey Pepper Chicken Tenders with 4-Cheese Mac & Cheese (53 grams of sugar) Pork Chop Chop Salad (California Pizza Kitchen) (68 grams of sugar) Salad with a Thai kick (51 grams of sugar)Napoleon French Toast with Syrup from the Cheesecake Factory (139 grams of sugar)

French Toast with a Bruleed Sauce (120 grams of sugar)Chili's:Waffles and Crispy Honey Chipotle (105 grams of sugar) Grilled Chicken in a Caribbean Salad (70 grams of sugar) Pepper Crisps (55 grams of sugar)Chipotle Honey Boneless Wings (40 grams of sugar) IHOP's Nutella Banana Crepes (67 grams of sugar) Pancakes made using Cinn-A-Stacks (60 grams of sugar) Grilled Chicken & Strawberry Salad at Longhorn Steakhouse (41 grams of sugar) Plantain-based Churrasco Steak (31 grams of sugar) 312 gram of sugar in a kids' fountain drink!Spicy Chicken, Gluten-free from P.F. Chang's (90 grams of sugar) Chicken that is sweet and sour (69 grams of sugar)Sichuan beef (67 grams of sugar)Yardhouse:Hot Chicken Nashville (75 grams of sugar) Chicken with Maui Pineapple (73 grams of sugar) Fries made with sweet potato (42 grams of sugar)What can you do to reduce your chances of eating too much sugar while you're out to eat?Here are some broad recommendations that have proven to be effective for me:Even if you're ordering a bacon-topped hamburger, tell your waitress you don't want any bread, chips, or croutons in your dish or on the table. Simply inform him or her that you do not eat certain foods and that they should be saved for someone else.Except on rare instances, avoid dessert. The majority of restaurant desserts include a lot of sugar. I know it doesn't seem enjoyable, but you'll be amazed how simple it becomes after a time to say "No" to dessert. You'll just lose your desire for them.If you're considering about purchasing a packaged, bottled, or wrapped food or beverage, read the Nutrition Facts label carefully, paying specific attention to the Total Sugars and Fiber content, as well as the serving size. Don't purchase it if the score isn't good.Many salad dressings include additional sugar, which might cause an insulin spike in an otherwise nutritious salad. Choose sugar-free or low-sugar options.Avoid fast food, which is often sugary, fiberless, and unhealthy, unless you've looked through their nutritional menu (online) and discovered something low in sugar, rich in fiber, and free of trans fat. It may take a few minutes, but you should be able to locate something that won't make your sugar belly any worse.Most of the time, I drink normal coffee. You may add milk if you want—I do it, and my biggest weakness right now is cappuccinos since I know there's lactose in them—but stay away from the sugar-laden espresso beverages seen at bistros and other establishments. Not soda, juice, or alcohol, but unsweetened water (except red wine in moderation). Order foods rich in healthy proteins (e.g., baked or grilled chicken, turkey, steak, eggs), fats (e.g., avocado, bacon, nuts, seeds), and carbohydrates (e.g., vegetables, fruits, and other high-fiber, low-sugar foods, such as Fiber Onecereal). Finally, don't overestimate your abilities or take too many risks. Before you eat anything, get all the information. If you feel a meal is excessive in sugar, don't order it or Google it to see what's going on. You can usually always discover enough nutritional information on the internet to help you make an educated choice about what you want to eat or drink.The first step in getting rid of your sugar gut is to eliminate as much sugar as possible from your diet. I realize how difficult it is to give up any trace of anything you like, and we all enjoy the taste of sugar, but there is aid on the way.Step two of the Sugar Belly Secret eases the pain and makes the whole get-healthy plan really practical, since you get to include delectable food choices that are prohibited in carb-Nazi diets, as long as they're rich in fiber.The easiest approach to achieve it is explained in Chapter 4.THE FOURTH PARTFiber is an important component.

I used to believe that fiber was only for the elderly and blocked up, but I was wrong. It's your undeniable advantage in the sugar belly battle.Fiber not only prevents sugar stomach, but it also allows you to consume far more delicious carbs than you would otherwise be able to consume without becoming overweight.Because fiber counteracts the effect of the extra carbs, many high-carb diets work effectively.Fiber, like a good man or woman, is becoming harder to come by.Food companies have removed all or nearly all fiber from a variety of foods because it reduces the timeframe of realistic usability, lengthens the time required to prepare and eat the food, and increases the cost of the product, none of which are beneficial to a global industry attempting to increase benefits and market share.As a result, we eat foods that are low in fiber and high in sugar, which is why the first two stages of a sugar stomach progression are primarily countermeasures—removing the extra sugar and increasing the fiber.It's really simple, but if you want to unprocess your eating routine, you'll need to stay alert and adjust your usage habits... Keep it real and honest.This was something I noticed recently while visiting two of the city's best supermarkets in Medellin, Colombia, where I am currently writing. Each time, I went looking for Fiber One (14 grams of fiber, 0 grams of sugar), my favorite high-fiber cereal, but it was nowhere to be found. Nothing came close to what I was looking for in terms of a comparable, possibly Colombian alternative. Every Nutrition Facts brand I looked at had a lot of added sugar and a lot of fiber.Only All Bran was available to me (12 grams of fiber, 9 grams of sugar). It's fine for occasional use because the fiber content is so high, but I prefer to eat cereal when it has a flavor that reminds me of a bite, and All Bran is surprisingly sweet. As a result, I was left empty-handed when I returned home.There are no issues to worry about. I stopped eating oats in Colombia—basically until I found an amazing one—and replaced them with higher-fiber breakfast foods. Even here in Medellin, it was not difficult to accomplish.Why is it so important to seek out, buy, and consume a variety of high-fiber foods? Because a high-fiber diet prevents a sugar belly, it's a good idea to eat a lot of fiber Fiber is your friend and ally in the battle against sugar indigestion. If you put it in play, it can help you dominate the Match of Hormones.Belly with FiberBy acting as a traffic cop in our intestines, fiber protects us from sugar.It works like this: Dissolvable solid fiber and insoluble solid fiber are the two types of solid fiber.A blend of solvent and insoluble fiber can be found in most plant-based foods and natural products.Fiber rushes to your digestive organs after you eat a sinewy food, creating a temporary roadblock for sugar and other carbs.Because insoluble fiber is harder, it acts as a rule boundary, while solvent fiber (which turns into a gel-like substance in the stomach) fills in the gaps.After that, they work together on three projects.To begin with, dissolvable and insoluble fiber divert a portion of the energy (sugar and other carbs) from our food to the gastrointestinal microorganisms that eat it, reducing carb assimilation into the rest of your body while allowing nutrients and micronutrients to pass through unhindered.Second, when these stringent traffic cops release other energy into our circulation system, they do so at a much slower rate (ensuring that it notices the lower speed limit), which protects our liver, pancreas, and mind from a sugar rush that would flood the body with fat-creating insulin.Third, because fiber reaches the end of the digestive system faster than everything else, it helps our brains receive the leptin ("satiety") signal sooner, making us feel full (satisfied), and reducing our desire for another serving.As a result, fiber reduces our absorption of fructose (which messes with the liver anyway) and other potentially filling carbs, reduces our insulin response, and improves leptin flagging, all of which help to prevent sugar belly.Fiber is a surprising cool material.That's why the quality of our calories, rather than the quantity, matters so much, and why calorie counting as a weight-loss strategy frequently fails.When you eat natural products, vegetables, and high-fiber complex carbs, your digestive microbes skip a large portion of the calories and dial back the rest, making them less likely to deliver sugar belly.Isn't it not a little pathetic?Isn't it true that organic product juice deserves a mention?It's easy to be fooled by outward appearances.Fruit juice fools the vast majority of people, including myself, for a long time, because it appears to be healthy. Who can say no to a glass of freshly squeezed orange juice?! Despite this, sugar is a Trojan horse.Because companies remove all or nearly all of the fiber from the natural product during processing, juices and smoothies can cause sugar gut.Juice causes anarchy in your digestion and contributes significantly to sugar belly without a sinewy designated spot to divert a portion of that sugar to your avaricious digestive microbes and dial back the rest.Your natural product should not be consumed. Instead, eat the whole organic product, which is stringy and full of flavor.FiberspottingLosing a sugar stomach necessitates advanced fiberspotting skills, but it's much easier than sugarspotting if you follow a few simple guidelines.First, check the number of grams of fiber in the food's Nutrition Facts label, as well as the amount of soluble and insoluble fiber. Food companies can't hide the ball as well as they can "Added Sugar." They must determine the amount and type of fiber in their named items, but you must notice and learn about it.It won't harm you if a food contains roughly the same amount of fiber as sugar. Keep looking in any case.Second, if a food or drink does not have a Nutrition Facts name and you don't know how many grams of fiber or added sugar it contains, search the internet for information.You'll frequently be able to locate the information you require quickly.Finally, if you're in a restaurant and can't rely on a Nutrition Facts name or a web search for healthy information, think twice. Invest some time to learn which foods contain fiber to balance out the (sweet) carbs you're eating and which don't. Then place your order for the delectable delicacies.Fruit juices and smoothies are to be avoided.Simply avoid organic fruit juices and smoothies unless you require a sugar rush.Prune juice is no exception. Prune juice contains a few grams of fiber, but it also contains an excessive amount of added sugar to make it beneficial, unlike most natural product juice. If all else fails, eat prunes. The situation has been resolved.foods of a light colorWhite rice, pasta, bread, and flapjacks and waffles made with white refined flour should be avoided from now on. That's a lot of privilege for a white person.White food varieties must be eliminated because they are frequently associated with processed, low-fiber foods that contribute to and exacerbate sugar belly.White potatoes, assuming you burn through the skin as well, are the most obvious possible special case for the general principle. I don't eat them very often because they're high in sugar and carbs (4.2 grams per potato), but they do provide a lot of fiber (8.9 grams) and protein (6.2 grams) to balance things out.Cereals that are high in sugar and low in fiberThe majority of cold oats contribute to a sugar stomach because they lack nearly enough fiber to balance out the extra sugar.Despite the fact that there are so many washouts to mention, some of the most heinous offenders include:Per cup, there are 15.69 grams of sugar and 0.9 grams of fiber, according to Quaker Oat's Cap'n Crunch.15 grams of sugar and 1 gram of fiber per cup of Kellogg's Honey Smacks 14 grams of sugar and 1 gram of fiber per cup in Post's Golden Crisp CerealSmorz cereal from Kellogg's has 13 grams of sugar per cup and 1 gram of fiber. General Mills Lucky Charms contain 12.6 grams of sugar and 1.8 grams of fiber per cup, Kellogg's Apple Jacks with Marshmallows contain 12 grams of sugar and 2 grams of fiber per cup, and Kellogg's Apple Jacks with Marshmallows contain 12 grams of sugar and 2 grams of fiber per cup, respectively.Honey produced by Quaker Oats Graham Oh's Cereal has 12 grams of sugar per cup but only 1 gram of fiber. Still haven't decided whether or not to stop eating it? Take a look: All of the oats listed above have more than 40% sugar in them (imagine the sugar shapes), and a few have more than half sugar, with Kellogg's Honey Smacks topping the list with 56.6 percent sugar... There's only one gram of fiber in the whole thing.Let's face it: If you're going to eat a crate of sugar, try not to smack it in the face.A Hostess Twinkie has 16 grams of sugar and no fiber, according to the method of examination. The cereals on my list are slightly better than that if you only eat one cup of cereal in the morning, but who does that?The majority of fast food restaurantsThe majority of low-cost food is low in fiber and high in added sugar, which is the recipe for sugar belly, and should be avoided at all costs.For example, McDonald's Hotcakes have 45 grams of sugar but only 2 grams of fiber. With or without the butter and syrup, they will make you fat.I could give you a thousand more examples of fast food that causes sugar belly, but the bottom line is this: If you're not sure about something, don't eat it. Expect to be the worst, and you'll almost always be right. You're in a fantastic position to go hungry for a while until you find some real food.We must, however, exercise caution. If you do your sugar-paunch research, you should be able to find at least one thing on any fast-food menu that isn't a dietary disaster, and a few that aren't too bad.Salad with Buttermilk and Bacon from McDonald's For example, 4 grams of fiber, 4 grams of sugar, and 33 grams of protein can be found in Crispy Chicken. I'm not sure what it tastes like, but if I had to eat at McDonald's, I'd order one of these with water or unsweetened coffee.All things considered, McDonald's excellent Egg McMuffin isn't bad. It has 2 g fiber, 3 g sugar, and 18 g protein. Last week, on my way to an event, I requested one and had no intention of wasting any time in devouring it.Observe and ConsumeDepending on the type of food you enjoy eating on a daily basis, there are a variety of ways to incorporate fiber for a sugar-stomach boost.Simply pick one or more high-fiber, low-sugar foods from the list below to ensure that you're burning through your carbs with fiber from one source or another.VegetablesLook, I'm not one of those people who adores vegetables, but some do taste better than others, and I eat them on a regular basis because they provide important micronutrients and sugar-fighting fiber.Fiber can be found in abundance in the following places:Green peas have 8.8 grams of fiber per serving, which is more than any other vegetable.when you boil a cup, When cooked, the parsnip (not to be confused with catnip) contains 7 grams of fiber per cup.When broccoli is boiled, it contains 5.1 grams of fiber per cup. When Brussels sprouts are boiled, they contain 4.1 grams of fiber per cup. When cooked, spinach has a fiber content of 4 grams per cup.Carrots have

2.3 grams of fiber per half-cup when cooked, while sweet corn has 3.6 grams per cup when boiled.FruitsRegardless of the regular sugar that comes with it, I love whole organic products as a rich source of fiber. I treat it as a treat and don't push myself too hard, but the ability to lose weight by eating products of the soil is pretty amazing.In the natural product category, there are a few all-stars to look out for:8 grams of fiber per cup of raw raspberries7.6 grams of fiber per cup of raw blackberriesAvocado– This superfood, which I used to despise but now adore, has 6.7 grams of fiber per cup. It's also nutrient-dense and high in healthy fats.Pears have 5.5 grams of fiber in their skin, so they're a good source of fiber.Apples have 4.4 grams of fiber in their skin, so they're a good source of fiber.Strawberries have 3.0 grams of fiber per cup, while bananas and oranges have 3.1 grams.Legumes, seeds, and nuts are some of the most nutritious foods you can eat.This diverse collection of foods packs a powerful fiber punch, and that's just the start. If you don't eat at least some of them on a regular basis, now is the time to begin.When split peas are boiled, they contain 16.3 grams of fiber per cup and are high in protein.When lentils are boiled, they contain 15.6 grams of fiber per cup.When cooked, black beans have 15 grams of fiber per cup, are high in protein and complex carbohydrates, and are extremely low in sugar (unlike sugary sweet baked beans).Chia seeds are a type of seed that comes from the– This is one of the most nutritious foods available. Every 1 ounce (approximately 2 tablespoons) serving contains 11 grams of fiber, 4 grams of protein, 9 grams of healthy fat, and numerous vitamins and antioxidants... They have a mild, nutty flavor that makes them versatile enough to be used in almost any recipe.Cooked or canned lima beans contain 9 grams of fiber per cup. Whole Quinoa – This superfood is often classified as a whole grain, but it's actually a seed, so I included it here to make seed-eating a little less intimidating. When cooked, it has a fiber content of 5 grams and no sugar.Amaranth – Amaranth is a grain-like seed, similar to quinoa. The fiber content per cup is 5.2 grams.3.5 grams of fiber per ounce (23 nuts), 2.9 grams of fiber per ounce (49 nuts), and 2.7 grams of fiber per ounce (pecans) (19 halves).Bran Cereal With High Fiber and Low SugarWheat grain can help you get more fiber in your diet if you choose the right kind. Shredded Wheat with no added sugar (with 6 grams of fiber and 0 grams of sugar per serving) and Fiber One (with 14 grams of fiber and 0 grams of sugar per serving) are my two favorites.Whole-grain bread with high fiberYou can eat bread if it comes from a high-fiber, low-added-sugar source, but proceed with caution.If you see "wheat," don't expect a high-fiber, low-sugar bread or grain item. Wheat bread is usually sweetened and shaded to make it appear better (and less handled) than it is. Breads labeled "light" should be avoided at all costs. oreven"higha slice of bread made with the fibers of an organization" Before you buy, check the mark!For example, here's a "Fit Integral" named Bimbo that I recently purchased in Medellin, Colombia, in the hopes of it living up to its moniker.As you can see, they wrote "0% Added Sugar" (in Spanish) right on the front of the package. I was intrigued, so I flipped it over to examine the Nutrition Facts label. It contains 2 grams of sugar per serving (2 cuts), as well as 4 grams of fiber and 10 grams of high-quality protein. That's quite impressive!In the United States, or wherever you are reading this, I'm confident you can find bread with less sugar and more fiber than mine. Whole Foods and Trader Joe's probably have better options, but I don't mind eating a few slices of Bimbo bread now and then.Whole grains that aren't sweetenedOatmeal – 4 grams of fiber when cooked; Brown or wild rice: Instead of white rice, use long-grain brown rice (1.8 grams of fiber per half cup when cooked) or wild rice.Low-Sugar Treats with a High Fiber ContentSome desserts strike a balance between fiber and sugar, allowing them to be consumed in moderation. As an illustration:Popcorn that has been air-popped is healthier than popcorn that has been buttered in a movie theater.3 cups of air-popped popcorn, on the other hand, contain almost no sugar (0.2 grams), no trans fat, and 3.6 grams of fiber per cup. Protein bars, in general, should be avoided because they're highly processed and the contents are difficult to decipher, but I admit to occasionally eating Quest protein bars. The Cookies and Cream, with 14 grams of fiber, 1 gram of sugar, and 21 grams of protein, is my personal favorite.Sugar Belly-Approved Treats – You can find a variety of treats that are high in fiber and low in sugar if you read the food labels and ingredient lists carefully. For example, I recently returned from a trip to a health food store in Medellin and brought home a few packs of my favorite Elemental protein treats. They have a variety of flavors, but my favorite is the Coconut Orange, which has 21.6 grams of protein, zero grams of sugar, and ten grams of fiber. They've added Stevia, but it still appears to be dead, so it'll be added to the list of things to fix.For me, this is acceptable.Tough Choices Whole Wheat Pasta – Think all pasta is off-limits due to its high carb content? Nope. You might be good to go if you choose the right whole-wheat pasta (6.3 grams of fiber when cooked) and the sugar level isn't too high. Just make sure you double-check the label.Sweet Potatoes with Skin: While sweet potatoes are high in vitamins and micronutrients, a single 130-gram sweet potato has 5.43 grams of sugar and only 3.9 grams of fiber. Although the fiber is beneficial, the amount of sugar in this product is excessive. If you have other options, think twice before laying one of these down.Is there a downside to incorporating fiber into the Sugar Belly Secret's second phase? It's true, but it's not a major issue.If you eat too much fiber, it can cause temporary swelling, gastrointestinal distress, and a lot of trips to the bathroom hours later.Rather than bombarding your body with a large portion of a case of Fiber One, start slowly and see how your body reacts.You should also expect something else, ahem, flatulence, regardless of how much fiber you add to your diet.Yes, exactly. Like the cows, you'll increase your carbon footprint by releasing a small amount of gas into the environment.Look at the bright side, though...Your sugar paunch will be literally flatulated away. Simply put, don't put too much effort into it, for your own sake... and mine.PART FIVERemove the booze.Back in the early days of P90X, my old pal and wellness master Tony Horton didn't drink alcohol, or so he claimed. With the rest of the posse, I went to a party to celebrate the completion of the P90X test group. Apart from Tony, who, surprisingly, didn't require it to have a good time, everyone was drinking beer or mixed drinks.Despite owning a strip club in Las Vegas and frequenting it, legendary fighter Floyd Mayweather is said to abstain from drinking alcohol.Do you want to completely give up booze in order to lose weight? There is no way.I have no intention of stopping because, like most people, I enjoy social drinking.Red wine is my go-to drink because it contains significant cell reinforcements and, when consumed in moderation, can actually prevent sugar tummy.I also notice that soft drink water with lime quenches my thirst, serves as an excellent substitute for liquor, and appears to be a genuine beverage, reducing peer pressure to consume.However, I will not lead anyone astray. In addition to red wine, I occasionally consume other types of liquor. I rarely drink excessively, but on rare occasions, I've been known to get a buzz.For example, a few months ago, I was invited to a large show in Medellin, Colombia, with a group of six people from my dance school, many of whom I didn't know very well. They were all drinking inexpensive Colombian brews, which a member of the gang was buying for them all. When all else was equal, I considered declining and drinking filtered water, but I couldn't. It was a once-in-a-lifetime opportunity to make new friends in a foreign country with similar interests, and I would have preferred not to be a downer or the odd man out.I kept a responsible attitude about it the next day, but I didn't let it ruin my day. I immediately re-boarded the sugar-gut cart and stayed put.Nobody is perfect, and any weight-loss plan that demands perfection is absurd and unrealistic for almost everyone.Smarter DrinkingYou're already ahead of the game if you don't consume alcohol under any circumstances. If you prefer, you can skip to the next section and skip this one.If you're like me and enjoy drinking socially, you don't have to quit cold turkey to lose weight. All you have to do now is drink more intelligently.

Believe it or not, a tiny amount of alcohol every day may help prevent weight gain and metabolic problem, especially if your beverage of choice is red wine, but it must be used in moderation.The problem stems from the over use of mixed drinks. Whether you're banging it in sync one and two of this technique, drinking excessively causes sugar midsection (or girth) and metabolic issue.Nowadays, an alarmingly big number of people use alcohol excessively, and it is evident.According to two large public surveys, the number of people diagnosed with alcoholism increased by almost 49 percent in the United States between 2001-2002 and 2012-2013, affecting 12.7 percent of the population.That means that around 1 in every 8 Americans is now an alcoholic. By the same token, no one should abstain from consuming alcoholic beverages. According to Detox.net's latest analysis of Americans:Even if it meant saving the life of a stranger, 36% of men and almost 26% of women said they wouldn't give up alcohol for life.Nearly a third of daily drinkers say they wouldn't stay with their partner if they didn't agree with their drinking habits. 47.5 percent would sooner give up coffee for a month than drink alcohol, 37.6% would rather give up sweets for a month than drink alcohol, and 17.1 percent would rather give up sex for a month than drink alcohol. andFor less than $365,458, the typical individual would not give up drinking forever.You don't have to completely give up alcohol or sweets. Simply take away a part of each and replace it with fiber to get the results you want.Select Your Poison: Alcohol or FructoseAlcohol (also known as ethanol) and fructose both make you fat, which is why sugar stomach and intestines are so closely linked.Sugar is matured to produce ethanol.Our minds utilize a little amount of ethanol to give us a buzz (or make us tipsy) when we eat anything, but our liver performs the real job, and consuming ethanol surpasses everything else, even any stored fat that your body may have ingested in some manner.Ethanol, in a sense, defers fat consumption till later.The same is true for whatever fructose you consume; however, every single bit of it is used by your liver. The rest of your body need nothing.it has to do with it in any way.Why do ethanol and fructose go straight towards the liver?Because it is where poisons and pseudo-poisons are used by the human body. As a result, you have the option of choosing between poison, booze, or fructose.They both skew the hormone game by assaulting your liver and triggering a chain reaction that causes you to gain weight.Because part of it is metabolized instantly in the cerebrum, alcohol is more dangerous (and seems to be more fun) than fructose. While excessive sugar consumption will not cause immediate injury or death, consuming an excessive amount of alcohol at one time might cause serious or even long-term harm to your body. The tales have all been told.However, keep in mind that, in the long run, excessive sugar and booze consumption produce a significant number of comparable actual medical disorders, remembering weight for the kind of sugar paunch, girth, or a combination thereof.That's why eliminating them from your diet is such a good idea.The Best Red Wine Is...Red wine, when used in moderation, has a number of health advantages. Red wine provides 9.4% of your daily potassium intake, 5% of your magnesium intake, and 4-9 percent of your iron intake, to name a few nutrients.It also includes healthy cell reinforcements like flavonoids and neoflavonoids, and one of the neoflavanoids, resveratrol (a molecule derived from grape skin), may help you lose belly fat, reduce bloating, fight cancer, and reduce your risk of heart disease.(Hint: Among red wines, Pinot Noir has the highest concentration of resveratrol.) So, unless you have a strong preference for anything else, go with Pinot Noir.)Isn't it cool?Although both white and red wine contain resveratrol, red wine has a higher concentration due to the extended fermentation time with the grape skins. Furthermore, red wine has a lower fructose content (0.5 to 1 gram per glass).We prefer it better in harmony with one of our cycles than white wine (1.25 to 1.5 grams per glass).Are you tired of drinking red or white wine but still want to get the advantages of resveratrol? All things considered, have a glass of sparkling wine. Because red and white grapes are used to make sparkling wines, such as Champagne from France, Prosecco from Italy, and Cava from Spain, they contain resveratrol. They also include polyphenol cell reinforcements, which aid to lower the risk of coronary artery disease and stroke by slowing the departure of nitric corrosive from the bloodstream.Although many sparkling wines have no more sugar than red wines, others add sugar to soften the harshness or provide a more balanced taste. For example, Brut Zero and Brut Nature have no added sugar and just around 0.5 to 1 gram per glass, while Prosecco has about 1 gram. Demi-Sec sparkling wine, on the other hand, has about 8 grams (1 to 2 teaspoons of added sugar) each glass. Make an informed request.In general, sparkling wine causes more headaches and migraines than regular wine, especially after the first glass or two. I'm not sure why, but it does.Finally, dessert wine should never be confused with red, white, or sparkling wine. According to the USDA, each glass of dessert wine has 8 grams of sugar, although many brands contain much more. For instance, 17 grams of sugar are included in a glass of Moscato.Please don't drink any sweet wine.So, in an ideal world, how much red, white, or sparkling wine should you consume?To become more fit, limit your use to a couple of glasses a few nights a week. It would be excellent if it were toned down, especially for women and children.I understand that a glass or two isn't much, and I'm not expecting you to punish yourself if you sometimes blow it while maintaining your attention.Simply do what you can, appreciate water between drinks (to combat dehydration and make you feel full), and remember that drinking moderately will help you smooth out your sugar belly much quicker.The outcome was mixed.This is what happens whenever you drink a cocktail that isn't red wine:Similarly to fructose, the worst of the sugars, the ethanol in your drink damages your liver, metabolism, and sugar belly. Whereas 100% of the fructose you eat goes straight to your liver since it's a poison, roughly 80% of the ethanol in an alcoholic drink goes straight to your liver. The remaining 10% is processed by various organs, including your brain, which gives you the "buzz."Alcohol is converted straight into visceral, sugar-belly fat, much like fructose, and produces most of the same damaging consequences in your Game of Hormones, including insulin resistance, leptin resistance, and metabolic syndrome.That's not a pretty image, but if you're going to drink drinks other than red wine—and I understand that the majority of you will, at some point—don't add a sweet blender to your drink for gods sakes.One of the most absurd things you can do to lose weight is to mix tonic, organic product juice, or a sweet soft drink into your cocktail.All things considered, you may drink your bourbon straight or mixed with soft drink water. So, what's the difference now? One of the most significant.The majority of alcohol consumed in its pure form includes no or very little sugar. Your body does need to use the ethanol, which will convert to fat in high amounts, but the problem ends there.When you mix your beverage with tonic, organic product juice, or a sweet soda, you've added a ton of sugar, especially fructose, which will strike your liver alongside the ethanol like a one-two punch... This will unquestionably put you on the verge of being overweight.If you want to get some resveratrol and other health benefits from a drink other than (red) wine, go for something at the top of the list:Beverage with alcohol (by the glass) sugar grams (Approx.)Vodka, gin, bourbon, rum, and tequila are examples of distilled/hard/straight liquors.Don't mix distilled/hard liquor with sweet liqueurs, which typically have about 10 grams of sugar in them.Caution: To sweeten the rum, some makers use sugar. In Medellin, Colombia, for example, there is a brand named "Year Extra Anejo." It tastes fantastic, but it is most likely because to the added sugar, which is one of the reasons I no longer drink it.a glass of vodka and a glass of soda0–0.5 gallons of beerCaution! Because they're low in sugar, don't get too enthusiastic and go pounding a few beers. When all other factors are equal, it's true that drinking a beer is preferable than many other alcoholic drinks that contain more sugar (including cider beers), but be cautious. Beer drinkers often fail to drink in moderation, which is terrible for any form of alcohol use, and alcohol promotes hunger and insulin release, causing your Game of Hormones to be messed up. Beer drinkers are also known to eat sugary, low-fiber "bar" cuisine such as pizza, wings, and other fried dishes, as well as unhealthy snacks.Wine (red) Champagne (0.5 to 1.0) (Brut Nature, Extra

Brut, and Brut) Prosecco White wine (1.0 %) Aguardiente Liquor (1.5 to 1.75 oz.) 2Sweet Champagne (Extra Dry, Dry, Sec, and Demi-Sec) is much sweeter than other varieties and should be avoided.12 Jägermeister (a shot) Daiquiri 3.4 Croft Original Sherry14 to 18 oz. gin-and-tonicOld Fashioned Bourbon Cocktail15 Mule Moscow 16–21 Martini 15 Whiskey Sour17 to 31 Margarita (depending on the contents and glass size) Irish cream Bailey's (3.38 ounces) 20.5 Cosmopolitan 22 Bulmers Original Cider 2039 to 60 Long Island Iced Tea (depending on glass size)Crisp Apple24 from Angry Orchard (Hard Cider)25 to 37 oz. Mojito (depending on glass size)Coca-Cola and Rum Pina Colada (27.5-30) (contingent upon glass size) Vodka Cranberry (27.5% to 43%)33 Strawberry Daiquiri 30 Strawberry Daiquiri 30 Strawberry Daiquiri 30 Strawberry Mike's Hard Lemonade is a brand of hard lemonade created by Mike. 32 Coke and Jack (nineteen)These were something I used to consume on a regular basis. It's no longer the case. Sixty LokoBefore we go on to the last chapter, here's one more hint:Consider a modest scale fast to make things right if you drink excessively on a particular day. My primary event is that. For roughly 12 hours, I don't eat and just drink water and espresso (counting 8 hours of sleep).When you go on a modest or irregular fast and deprive your accumulation of food, your body enters a ketogenic state and begins to consume stored fat.This is the foundation for the Ketogenic diet. It's a fantastic way to get in shape quickly, and some people rely on it, but it's not a long-term, practical solution for my sugar paunch, and it's uncomfortable. I prefer not to participate.I don't need to track and reduce carbohydrates so drastically, nor do I need to worry about calories or portion sizes if I follow three simple steps: eliminate sugar, increase fiber, and eliminate alcohol.That's the Sugar Belly Secret to lasting, healthy weight loss, but you can also get twice results by doing something else I enjoy: exercising.However, Chapter 6 will explain why I strongly recommend that you include at least some kind of movement in your get-healthy strategy. However, Chapter 6 will explain why I strongly recommend that you include at least some kind of movement in your get-healthy strategy.SECOND PARTExercise a second time.Only a few people are aware of the facts behind my P90X experience.I honestly would not have made it through the first 30 days, much alone appear as a cast member in one of the P90X recordings and an early example of conquering hardship in infomercials, if I hadn't immediately adjusted my eating habits to something similar to the Sugar Belly Secret.Years ago, on the first day of the P90X test group in Santa Monica, CA, I knew my frail, 41-year-old body (which included a constant bad back and fluctuating levels of sciatic nerve torment) wouldn't be able to withstand 90 days of intense exercise if I got hurt or debilitated along the way, and I was determined not to let either of those things happen.However, within the first 10 to 14 days of the treatment, I was effectively self-destructing. When I brought this up with Tony Horton (the P90X creator who was teaching the classes) and a few others, they immediately recognized that my eating routine at the time—I was eating like an average, stressed lawyer—wasn't enough and suggested that I either cook at home or order new, natural food from a nearby food delivery service.I started paying an organization to deliver all of my suppers and snacks to my legal office for the remainder of the program since I wasn't going to start cooking and I didn't want to embarrass myself by being one of the first to terminate the experimental group. (Beachbody, the company that created P90X, did not have its own meal delivery service.)That was, without a doubt, the wisest decision I've ever made.I instantly felt and looked better, and the results were outstanding:My weight fell from 181 to 173 pounds, my body fat fell from 14.3% to 8.7%, and my waistline shrank from 33 to 30 inches.Isn't it awesome? Actually, it's not. In contrast to the Day 1 snapshot, I may not seem slim in the Day 90 photograph above since it was taken after my final full-body activity when I was puffed up. I'm almost 6'2" tall, and throughout P90X, I wanted to drop some belly fat, but I assumed I'd replace it with more muscle, rather than down to 173 pounds.I was in good shape, but I hadn't gained enough muscle to compensate for my fat reduction.

P90X isn't adjusted, to be honest. Although it's a one-size-fits-all DVD (and now Internet) workout program with variable outcomes, I learned the hard way that 173 pounds—six pack or no six pack—is not a good look on someone my height. I don't know how I'd express it. Allow me to share a little anecdote with you.I went to a pub in Santa Monica, CA with another individual who'd just done the program two or three days after the P90X test group concluded, hoping to see a gorgeous English young girl. I'd had a strong desire for her for a long time but had little to show for it, but I hoped that with my new P90X physique, that would change. It would have been my night if it hadn't been for the fact that I had to workWhen she approached me, I was leaning against the bar, and I saw her walk slowly toward me. It was a one-of-a-kind movie. As she got closer, she seemed to be really gorgeous and thrilled to be there."What was the deal?" she said, her voice troubled. Is it safe to say you're in good shape? "Have you all perished?" "Day crazy home work out schedule," I said, taken aback. "This is the healthiest I've ever been."She didn't seem really interested. "However, you seem to be really emaciated, like if you are ill or something." It is something I strive to stay away from. You want to eat and drink more often again. Sorry... Bartender!"That was an unpleasant experience. I really cared about this young girl and tried all of the P90X bands in vain, or at least that's how it seemed. I looked into her eyes even closer.I wish I could say I handled the disappointment with maturity, but I didn't. I walked out after making an insensitive, overly cautious remark.I apologized some days later. She kindly forgave me, said she understood, and offered an explanation that went something like this: "Please accept my apologies." Your feelings were wounded by what I said. That was not my intention. You appear appealing in overall. It's only that seeing you reminded me of a great friend who died recently of AIDS."Ouch. AIDS?!This time I handled it better, but it still felt like a slap in the face.I practice the Sugar Belly Secret 5 or 6 times a week to stay fit and healthy these days, but I don't overdo it. I don't have to put up with wacky workout routines, andYou don't, either.Let it all out if you're a fan of P90X, Insanity, CrossFit, or anything. I'm not trying to discourage you, but you can get rid of your sugar belly without them.Indeed, presuming that you exercise to burn calories rather than to improve the quality of those calories is a recipe for failure.Consider the scenario. A regular average guy would have to run for 2 hours and 21 minutes or walk for 4 hours and 38 minutes to burn off the calories in a McDonald's Big Mac, gigantic fries, and giant Coke. In addition, a regular sized women would need to undertake nearly 2 hours of yoga or 46 minutes of cycling to burn off the calories in a Starbucks Venti Java Chip Frappuccino combined espresso and 2 percent milk.Do you think that's a viable weight-loss strategy? Hardly.Don't worry about tracking calories. The Sugar Belly Secret will help you control the type of your calories. Add exercise to your regular routine if you want to flatten your tummy quicker and enhance your general health and fitness. It burns fat, improves insulin sensitivity, builds strong muscle, and, perhaps most importantly, reduces stress (cortisol) during a time when most of us could use a little more peace, lightheartedness, and happiness.Sense the HeatIf you don't cut sugar, increase fiber, and eliminate alcohol from your diet, exercise won't help you lose weight, but if you do it right, it may help you lose weight and get rid of sugar.For instance, here's a tried-and-true sugar-paunch hack:On an empty stomach, do some kind of cardiovascular activity for 30 minutes first thing. You may drink espresso or water before to the event, but no smoothies or food.Because of this, it produces the desired result:You've successfully fasted for 8 hours or whatever long you slept when you wake up in the morning. As a result, your body lacks a ready-to-use carbohydrate supply.to utilize as a source of energy while starting to practice before eating As a result, it uses your stored fat as fuel.This fat-consuming criterion is critical to the low-carb Ketogenic diet, and there's no better time to put it into practice than first thing in the morning.Are you a night owl? There are no issues to worry about. Plan B is in the works.Working exercise later in the day burns fat, but not as rapidly or as efficiently as working out first thing in the morning.Additionally, any kind of activity builds muscle, which, like your liver and stomach, eats fat stored around the actual muscles. It also improves insulin sensitivity, resulting in lower insulin levels, which is exactly what you want since too much insulin causes weight gain.Exercise burns both subcutaneous (enormous butt) and instinctual (intra-organ or sugar tummy) fat.Visceral fat poses a greater threat to your health and well-being since it accumulates in places where it doesn't belong– most notably, your waistline– and causes inflammation, insulin resistance, corpulence, metabolic disorder, and a long list of potentially harmful illnesses and disorders.But there's a bright lining: visceral fat burns quickly when you become fit—truth be told, your sugar paunch will recoil before your massive butt— and it responds well to regular activity that raises your heart rate.Subcutaneous fat, on the other hand, is better and more difficult to shed, but regular exercise may help. It will give you even more drive to complete the task.BoostWhy couldn't I build enough muscle during the P90X test to compensate for my fat loss and maintain a healthy weight?Except if the calorie counter does the necessary exercise to keep up with and build muscle along the way, diets typically result in a deficiency of more muscle than fat.I was completing the Shoulders and Arms workout and other exercise regimens to build muscle, but I was also losing muscle by eating less carbohydrates and doing substantially more rigorous cardio than was recommended. (If you've tried P90X Plyometrics before, you'll understand what I'm talking about.)In retrospect, I would have done better if I had done more serious weightlifting and less exercise, and eaten much more high-quality food to help prevent muscle deterioration, but I was learning on the job, just like everyone else. In a test group, this is what happens.Some things are successful, while others are unsuccessful. You do everything you can, you pray for divine intervention, and you do everything you can.as well as learning from your blundersI'm grateful for my P90X change and hope it doesn't sound strange, but I'm not allowing myself to be transformed into a wiped out leave figure with abs by eating less junk food or increasing my cardiovascular activity.Instead, I supplement the Sugar Belly Secret with exercise to build muscle while burning fat at a steady, sustainable rate, and I sincerely hope that you do the same... whether or not you have to. But there's one more reason to exercise, and it's ostensibly the most important: it lowers blood pressure (cortisol) more effectively than anything else, or so I believe.I wish you peace.My transformation from P90X Joe to Average Joe began with dizziness a few weeks before my first session and accelerated while working as a patent case expert in South Florida in a highly stressful environment.It started out as interesting work, and the organization grew rapidly during my residency, but it soon became abnormal for everyone except the chief, who didn't improve as a result of his success. I did everything

I could to avoid thinking about it in that way, but going to work was stressful sooner or later.For the time being, I didn't self-destruct, but I was slowly letting go. I stopped working out regularly and ate insufficiently. I worked erratic, long hours and didn't get enough sleep. It was also visible from top to bottom. I was pale, drained, and chubby, and I was very upset about it.I'm on the verge of giving up.But then I quit my job.It wasn't easy giving up the pay and benefits to become a hopeful creator and maker, but it was one of the best decisions I've ever made. Life is far too short to consider tolerating a completely unappealing workplace if there is a viable alternative, which there almost always is, regardless of how risky it is to reach it.I'm sure you've dealt with similar situations in your own life, assuming there haven't been any more traumatic events, and you understand the inclination, whether the stress stemmed from business, financial, or personal issues. (For example, adjusting to the loss of a friend or family member, especially a child, is obviously far more difficult.)Obviously, we can't eliminate all stress from our lives, and sometimes it's just a kick in the pants that motivates us to do something brave, meaningful, or extraordinary. However, if we do not respond appropriately and effectively to stress, it can be fatal.As you may recall from our discussion in Chapter 2, cortisol is your stress hormone in the Game of Hormones, and high levels of cortisol cause insulin resistance (that is, an excess of fat-producing insulin), the consumption of comfort foods, and the accumulation of sugar-gut fat, all of which increase the risk of weight gain, metabolic disease, and premature death.And, like I did, you can retaliate by reducing your stress levels through contemplation, yoga, more rest, or even quitting a bad job.That's all well and good, but exercise reduces stress and the subsequent arrival of cortisol into your system more effectively, economically, and effectively than anything else, and you gain additional benefits—fat loss, muscle gain, and improved appearance—as a side benefit.Another point of view suggests that physical activity can help you to be more self-controllable when it comes to avoiding sugary foods and beverages. Researchers are still trying to figure out why this happens, but I imagine that those who practiced were less likely to be worried and reach for comfort food.Isn't it incredible? Certainly.Reducing stress through exercise will help you execute the Sugar Belly Secret more effectively, naturally, and consistently, while also making you feel better, more grounded, and more attractive.ConclusionIt's a great time to stop responding to your sugar belly with fad diets, exercise programs, gym equipment, and weight loss medical procedures that only produce short-term results and long-term disappointment. Such yo-yo results can lead to feelings of inadequacy and self-doubt, and the hassle can be nearly as bad as not trying at all.There is a new, normal, basic, proactive system for getting thinner and permanently changing your life, as this book has demonstrated.You don't have to obsess over calorie counting, carbs, or healthy fats, or even exercise.And, unlike me, you're not stuck with an unfortunate sugar tummy or a debilitating metabolic condition for the rest of your life because you're currently overweight, corpulent, old, debilitated, or losing your edge.Right now, you can start losing weight and getting rid of your sugar belly.All you need to do is follow three simple steps to change your eating habits:Subtract sugar from the equation, add fiber, and subtract alcohol from the equation.The Sugar Belly Secret is as follows:In the grand scheme of things, you don't need to completely eliminate sugar and alcohol from your diet. Although losing weight would be ideal, this system does not necessitate perfection or extreme measures.All things considered, you do not need to consume fiber throughout the day. A little goes a long way, and too much fiber will send you to the bathroom for a rude awakening. (If you try too hard on the fiber, amigos, your body will tell you.)While I haven't spent much time talking about "fats," it is implied that you should avoid phony, processed "trans fats." I didn't devote a section to it because it's become common knowledge, and food companies have effectively begun to exclude it from the majority of their products.Stick to real foods like avocado, nuts, cheddar, bacon, and coconut oil, and you'll be fine.When you realize that food and beverage companies have degraded our food supply by adding massive amounts of sugar and removing fiber from nearly everything, you'll notice that you'll eat less often.You can do the opposite covertly and quickly reverse the situation.If you believe that some government office will intervene and persuade organizations to provide better food, think again. There's a lot of money to be made or saved by keeping the unpleasant truth hidden from you, and it's a lot easier to blame you for not being shrewd or restrained enough to solve the problem than to make it easier for you to do so.It's up to you to outsmart the system, but with the Sugar Belly Secret, you can do it and reap the benefits for a lifetime.Reducing sugar consumption lowers insulin resistance, while increasing fiber intake lowers fat-production insulin surges. Finally, drinking less alcohol or making more informed choices in this regard (red wine in particular) helps your body spend more energy consuming fat and less time storing it.When you begin to "un-handle" your eating routine by adding fiber while reducing sugar and alcohol, you will notice and feel the difference. You'll be eating real food and beverages with more calories, which will normally lead to weight loss, after only a few simple changes to your current eating routine.And here's the best part: The Sugar Belly Secret is remarkably simple, practical, and manageable. That is why, in my opinion, it is the best long-distance option.The best arrangement is one you can stick to, as the saying goes, and this one is one you can stick to.

Adding and subtracting should be simple.If you want to speed up and boost your results while also building some lean, fat-burning muscle and lowering your blood pressure, you can do so by doing something else: exercising. Exercise is optional, but it can help you lose weight.Impeccably keep your secret. It is up to you to make the decision.By making a few minor changes to the way you eat and live, you can allow the Sugar To Midsection Secret to do something extraordinary in a natural, practical way.You can choose to ignore it and continue doing things that don't work for you in the long run and will never work for you.I respect your decision if you don't want to try my new weight-loss system right now, but I believe I've planted a seed that will grow into something special someday. The Sugar Belly Secret is based on clues left by successful people.I make mistakes all the time, but I also pay attention to what successful people do, learn from them, and follow in their footsteps when it makes sense. I enjoy doing whatever I want, but there is no need for me to waste time. I'd rather stay on goliaths' shoulders and invite others to join me up there. That is why I have written this book.

Taking the most elite low-carb and high-carb abstentions from food and refining everything down to what truly matters is the Sugar Belly Secret. Many of these diet plans are effective. In any case, I'm not making any claims, and I'm a big fan of Keto and other low-carb diets. They're too difficult, extreme, complicated, and potentially dangerous to be a long-term solution, though.The Sugar Belly Secret is a one-of-a-kind method for getting rid of belly fat. It's more concerned with long-term improvements in your health, wellness, and appearance than with fleeting intercessions that give you a taste of success before snatching it away, and I tried my hardest to explain it as clearly as I could.I sincerely hope you found this book interesting, because there's no reason why we shouldn't have fun together along the way. This is not a bombing mission over Vietnam; it's a health-improvement plan.Furthermore, worrying about your sugar stomach will exacerbate the problem. Katherine ("Kitty") Howe, my left grandma, was the cutest and most amazing person I'd ever met.It didn't take long for everyone to notice and feel her exceptionality. "Gram, what's the key to life?" I asked one day at her house. "Gracious... be glad and snicker a lot!" she said recently, chuckling and briefly considering everything.I had a smidgeon of cynicism. Isn't that all? It dawned on me at that point. She cultivated a proclivity for giggling and happiness by thinking and living that way.I've always remembered it and try to avoid losing my sense of humour or satisfaction, especially when it comes to important things like eating, drinking, and exercising.Perhaps this explains why the Sugar Belly Secret works.For me, this is admirably. It isn't simple, consistent, ordinary, or long-term.With a snicker and a smile, you can get in shape, build muscle, and improve your overall health and well-being.So, are you ready to get rid of that muffin top?"Hagale pues!" as the locals say. (Then go ahead and do it! I'll be right there with you every step of the way, guiding you toward a successful conclusion.

CPSIA information can be obtained
at www.ICGtesting.com
Printed in the USA
LVHW061242260322
714287LV00016B/257